Claim Your FREE Resources T
Becoming The Woman You
Visit www.ivacrawford.syste
Get Access.

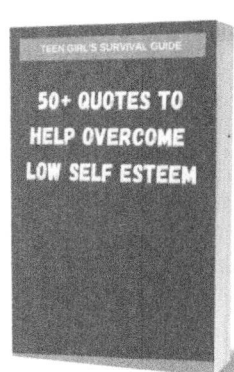

Claim Your FREE Resources That Will Help You in Becoming The Woman You Need to Be. Kindly Visit www.ivacrawford.systeme.io/63885be9 to Get Access.

10+ Easy Jobs for Teen Girls,
This book is perfect for teenage girls looking to make some extra money. It provides 10+ easy job ideas that can be done from home or in the local area. From babysitting to pet care, this book is full of ideas to help teens make money while learning valuable life skills. It also includes tips on how to market yourself and how to stay safe when working. Teens will be sure to find the perfect job to help them achieve their financial goals.

10+ Simple Breathing Exercises to Help Combat Stress and Anxiety
This book provides 10+ simple breathing exercises that can help combat stress and anxiety.
Each exercise is designed to help you relax and focus on the present moment. With these exercises, you can find relief from the stress and anxiety that can be present in everyday life.

10+ Simple Workouts for Teen Girls
This book offers 10+ straightforward and simple workouts for teenage girls. Each exercise is designed to help tone, strengthen, and shape the body, while providing fun and effective results. Exercises range from beginner to advanced levels. With this book, you can follow a variety of workouts to help you look and feel your best. Perfect for teenage girls who want to live a healthy and active lifestyle.

100+ Quotes to Help Overcome
100+ Quotes to Help Overcome Anxiety is a powerful collection of inspirational words to help people affected by anxiety. It includes over 100 quotes from famous people, philosophers, and everyday people who have faced and conquered the challenges of anxiety. Whether you are feeling overwhelmed, stressed, or simply looking for words of encouragement, this book will provide you with the support and insight needed to take back control of your life.

50+ Quotes to Help Overcome Low Self Esteem
Quotes to Help Overcome Low Self Esteem" is a collection of inspiring words and phrases to help readers build confidence and self-worth. Through uplifting quotes from some of the world's most influential figures, this book provides unique motivation and guidance to help readers overcome their low self-esteem and reach for their dreams.

CLAIM YOUR FREE RESOURCES!!!

Teen Girl's Survival Guide

How to be confident, make friends easily, set boundaries, prepare yourself for your future, and everything you need to know

By

Iva Crawford

Copyright © 2022 Iva Crawford, All Rights Reserved

No portion of this book may be copied, saved in a database, or communicated using any technology, including but not limited to photocopying, recording, scanning, or electronic methods.

This book is a work of nonfiction. The names, characters, places, and events are either a product of the author's imagination or are used fictitiously. Any likeness to real people, living or dead, businesses, occasions, or locations is purely coincidental.

Published in the United States of America.

Reproduction in whole or in part and in any format is permitted, but all rights are reserved

Legal Notice

This book is protected under copyright law. No part of this book may be reproduced, transmitted, stored, or distributed in any form or by any means, electronic, mechanical, photocopying, recording, or otherwise, without the prior written permission of the copyright holder. All rights are reserved.

Disclaimer

The views and opinions expressed in this book are solely those of the author and do not necessarily reflect the official policy or position of any other entity. Any content provided by the author is of their opinion, and is not intended to malign any religion, ethnic group, club, organization, company, or individual. The author is not responsible for the consequences of any decisions taken by readers on the basis of information provided in this book. No responsibility or liability will be accepted by the author for any losses, damages, or injuries resulting from the use or misuse of any information contained within this book.

Contents

I. 1
Introduction: What is a Teen Girl's Survival Guide? 1

II. 4
Building Confidence and Self-Esteem 4
    Developing Positive Self-Talk 6
    Embracing and Appreciating Yourself 8
    Body Image 10

III. 13
Navigating Reproductive Health: A Step-by-Step Guide to Understanding Your Body 13
    A. Puberty and Its Effects 13
        Physical Changes 14
        Emotional Changes 19
    B. Understanding Menstruation And How to Prepare For It 20
        What is the Menstrual Cycle? 20
        How to Check Your Menstrual Cycle 21
        How to Prepare for Your Period 23

IV. 25
Making Friends and Connecting with Others 25

Developing Social Skills 27
Navigating Social Media 30
V 33
Dealing with Peer Pressure 33
Recognizing Negative Influences 35
Creating Healthy Boundaries 38
VI 41
Overcoming Challenges and Difficult Situations 41
Identifying Your Strengths 43
Developing Coping Strategies 45
VII 49
Preparing for Your Future 49
Setting Goals 51
Creating a Plan for College and Beyond 53
Conclusion 56

I

Introduction: What is a Teen Girl's Survival Guide?

I was just a teenager when I started to realize how tough life could be. I had a lot of dreams and ambitions, but navigating through life as a teenage girl was a challenge. I was a bright and ambitious girl, but I was naive and often fell into the wrong crowds, accepted poor advice, and made bad decisions.

At first, I was just trying to fit in and have fun. I had parties, dated the wrong guys, and spent way too much money. I was living life to the fullest, but I was not setting myself up for success. I was being reckless and care free, without realizing that I would soon regret my choices.

As I got older, I started to see the consequences of my actions. I had gone down a destructive path, and I was struggling to get out of it. I started to realize that I had been making a lot of mistakes and that I had to make a change.

I started by taking responsibility for my actions. I made a list of all the mistakes I had made and then worked to make up for them. I worked hard to fix my relationships with family and friends, and I made sure to focus on my studies and my goals. I slowly started to build myself back up and create a better life for myself.

It took a lot of hard work, but eventually I was able to turn my life around. I was able to get back on track and start making better decisions. I was able to stay focused on my goals and build a bright future for myself.

I am now a successful young woman, but I will never forget the struggles I faced as a teenage girl. I am passionate about helping other young girls avoid the mistakes I made. I want to be an example and show them that they can make better decisions and create a bright future for themselves. I want to help them see that they don't have to live recklessly and that they can make the right choices to set themselves up for success.

Welcome to the Teen Girls Survival Guide! This guide is designed to help teenage girls navigate the challenges and opportunities of their teenage years. I understand that this can be a difficult time of transition, and I want to provide you with the tools and resources to help you make the most of this period in your life.

This guide will address a wide range of issues that teen girls commonly face – from body image and mental health to relationships and managing stress. I will provide you with valuable insight and advice on dealing with these issues, as well as practical tips on how to stay safe and healthy.

Most importantly, I want to provide you with the support and guidance to help you feel empowered, confident, and capable of achieving your goals – both now and in the future. I am here to help you take control of your life, and to make sure you have all the resources you need to make this journey a successful one.

I hope that this guide will serve as a valuable resource for teen girls and that it will enable you to make the most of your teenage years.

II

Building Confidence and Self-Esteem

Being a teenage girl can be a difficult and confusing time, with many challenges and changes to adjust to. It's important for teenage girls to build their confidence and self-esteem, as these will help them to be better prepared to face the challenges that lie ahead. Here are a few ways to help teenage girls build confidence and self-esteem.

First and foremost, it is important to be kind to yourself. It can be easy to be self-critical when faced with difficult situations, but it's important to remind yourself that you are doing your best, and that mistakes are part of the learning process. Even if you don't get the outcome you want, it's important to remember that you are capable and resilient.

Secondly, it's important to build a strong support system of family and friends that you can turn to when you need help or advice. Having a strong network of people who understand and care about you can be a great source of comfort and strength.

Thirdly, it's important to focus on your strengths rather than your weaknesses. Acknowledge and celebrate your successes, no matter how small, and don't be afraid to take risks. Taking on challenges and pushing yourself to reach your goals can help you to build confidence and self-esteem.

Fourthly, it's important to get involved in activities that you enjoy, whether it's a sport, a hobby or a club. Getting involved in something you're passionate about can help to boost your confidence and bring out the best in you.

Finally, it's important to take care of yourself. Eating a balanced diet, exercising regularly and getting enough sleep are all important for maintaining physical and mental health. Taking care of yourself can help to boost your self-confidence and self-esteem.

Overall, building confidence and self-esteem as a teenage girl can be a difficult process, but it is an important one. Taking the time to focus on yourself, to recognize your strengths and to build a strong support system can help to make the journey a little bit easier.

Developing Positive Self-Talk

As a teenage girl, it can be difficult to maintain a positive outlook on life. You are dealing with the physical and emotional changes of puberty, while also trying to manage school, friendships, and other activities. It's normal to feel overwhelmed or down on yourself at times. But, it's important to have positive self-talk to help you stay focused, motivated, and resilient. Here are some tips on how to develop positive self-talk as a teenage girl.

1. Acknowledge your feelings.

It's okay to feel anxious, angry, or sad. Acknowledging your feelings can help you to process them and move on. When you feel negative about yourself, don't bottle it up. Talk to a trusted friend or family member about it, or write down how you feel in a journal.

2. Replace negative thoughts with positive ones.

When negative thoughts come up, replace them with positive ones. For example, if you think "I'm not good enough", replace it with "I am capable and strong". This will help you to stay positive and focused on what's important.

3. Set realistic goals.

It's important to have goals to work towards. Make sure they are, however, both attainable and reasonable. Having sentiments of failure and disappointment as a result of setting unrealistic expectations.

4. Celebrate your successes.
Whatever your level of achievement, it's crucial to recognize and appreciate it. This will help to boost your self-esteem and confidence.

5. Focus on the present.

It is simple to become mired in regret or anxiety about the future. But, it's important to focus on the present and make the most of it.

6. Be kind to yourself.

It's important to be kind and forgiving towards yourself. Don't be too hard on yourself if you make a mistake.

By following these tips, you can develop positive self-talk and maintain a positive outlook on life. Try to focus on the positives and take each day as it comes. Remember, you are strong and capable, and you can do anything you set your mind to!

Embracing and Appreciating Yourself

As a teenage girl, it can be easy to forget to appreciate yourself and your own unique qualities. We often get caught up in comparing ourselves to others, which can lead to feelings of self-doubt and low self-esteem. However, there are plenty of ways to embrace and appreciate yourself as a teenage girl and feel confident in who you are. Here are a few methods for carrying it out.

1. Take time to focus on yourself. Make an effort to spend time focusing on yourself and the things you care about. This could be anything from going for a run or to the library, to just taking some time to relax and have some 'me time'.

2. Treat yourself. Taking care of yourself is important, so why not treat yourself every once in a while? Whether it's buying yourself a new outfit or going out for a nice meal, do something that makes you feel good.

3. Take care of yourself. Your physical and mental health should be taken care of. Assure yourself that you are getting enough sleep, eating a healthy diet, and exercising frequently.

4. Spend time with positive people. Assemble a support system of individuals who will boost your self-esteem.

5. Avoid negative self-talk. Instead of putting yourself down, focus on the positive things about yourself and your life.

6. Accept compliments. It can be hard to accept compliments, but it's important to remember that you deserve them.

7. Believe in yourself. Believe that you are capable of achieving whatever it is that you want to achieve in life.

8. Take risks. Push yourself out of your comfort zone and take risks. This could be anything from trying a new hobby to applying for that job you've been thinking of.

9. Celebrate your uniqueness. There is no one else like you, so embrace your own unique qualities.

10. Don't be afraid to make mistakes. Mistakes are part of life and can help you to learn and grow.

11. Take pride in your appearance. Be proud of how you look and dress in attire that makes you feel good about yourself.

These are just some of the ways to embrace and appreciate yourself as a teenage girl. By taking the time to focus on yourself, you can learn to love and appreciate who you are and develop a greater sense of self-confidence.

Body Image

Body image is something that is especially important to teenage girls. It's a time when they're growing and learning and discovering who they are and what they look like. It's a time of transition and a time of self-discovery. It's also a time when young women are especially vulnerable to the pressures of society and the media to conform to a certain "ideal" body type.

The pressure to look a certain way can be overwhelming for teenage girls. They might feel like they must be thin, fit, and perfect to be accepted, which can lead to low self-esteem and negative body image. It can also lead to unhealthy behaviors, such as crash dieting, excessive exercise, and disordered eating.

It's important for teenage girls to learn healthy ways to cope with the pressures of society and the media. Positive body image is an important part of self-esteem, and it's essential for young women to learn to love and accept themselves for who they are.

One way to foster a positive body image is to focus on health rather than size or shape. Instead of trying to achieve the "ideal" body type, teenage girls should focus on eating a balanced diet, getting regular exercise, and learning to appreciate their unique body shape.

It's also important for teenage girls to be aware of the media's influence on body image. Many of the images they see in magazines, television, and movies are heavily photo shopped and unrealistic. It's important to remember that these images aren't real, and to focus on developing a healthy body image instead.

Teenage girls should also remember that beauty comes in all shapes and sizes. Everyone is unique, and it's important to recognize and celebrate the beauty of all body types. Encouraging friends and family to do the same can help teenage girls to feel more confident and comfortable in their own skin.

Finally, it's important for teenage girls to talk about their body image. Talking to supportive friends and family, or seeking professional help if needed, can help them to develop a positive body image and learn to appreciate their own unique beauty.

Body image is an important issue for teenage girls, but it doesn't have to be a negative experience. By focusing on health, being aware of media influence, and talking about their body image, teenage girls can learn to appreciate their unique beauty and develop a positive body image.

III

Navigating Reproductive Health: A Step-by-Step Guide to Understanding Your Body

As a teenage girl, understanding your reproductive health is essential in order to make informed decisions about your body and your future. Reproductive health includes everything from puberty to contraception and sexually transmitted infections (STIs). It is important to be aware of the various changes that occur during puberty and how to properly care for your body during this time.

A. Puberty and Its Effects

Puberty is an important stage of development for teens, and it can be a confusing and sometimes difficult time for young women. As a teen girl, it is important to understand the physical, emotional, and social changes that will occur.

Physical Changes

These changes can range from the development of breasts and underarm hair to acne and mood swings. Understanding the physical changes that come with puberty can help teenage girls feel more prepared and in control of their bodies.

1. Growth Spurts

One of the most noticeable physical changes of puberty is an increase in height. This is due to a growth spurt that happens during puberty, which is caused by a rapid increase in the production of the hormone, testosterone. During this time, teen girls may find that they grow in height very quickly and unexpectedly. This growth spurt usually lasts for around two years and is usually complete by the time a teen girl reaches the age of 16 but can vary from girl to girl.

2. Breast Development

The development of breasts is another common physical change of puberty for teen girls. While every girl is different and experiences their own unique journey, the process of breast development usually follows a similar sequence.

The first stage of breast development usually begins between the ages of 8-13, when the nipples and surrounding area start to become more prominent and the breasts begin to form. During this stage, the breasts will be quite small, and may even appear a little uneven. It is perfectly normal for breasts to develop at different rates, and at this stage, they may not even look like they are growing.

The next stage usually starts around the age of 13-15, when the breasts start to grow more noticeably in size. During this stage, the nipples and areola become darker in color and larger. As the breasts continue to grow, they may also become more rounded and the nipples may become more raised. This is also a good time to start wearing a supportive bra, as this will help the breasts to develop properly and provide comfort.

The third stage begins around the age of 15-17, when the breasts are almost fully developed. At this stage, the breasts will have reached their full size and shape, and the nipples and areola will also be fully formed. During this stage, teenage girls may find that they need to wear a different size bra as their breasts continue to grow and develop.

3. Pubic and Body Hair

The development of pubic and body hair is another physical change of puberty for teen girls. For a young girl going through puberty, the process of pubic and body hair growth typically begins around the age of 8 or 9.

At first, it may start out as fine, light-colored hair, usually on the lower stomach, inner thighs, and around the genitals. As the girl continues to go through puberty, the hair will become darker and thicker, and eventually may cover the entire pubic area.

The growth of body hair usually starts a bit later than pubic hair, usually around the age of 10 or 11. This hair will typically start growing on the arms, legs, and underarms, and can eventually spread to other areas of the body such as the chest, back, and face. It is important as a young girl going through puberty to be aware of the process of pubic and body hair growth, so you can be prepared for the changes your body is going through. It is also important for you to understand that this is a perfectly normal process, and that everyone goes through it.

4. Skin Changes

As a teen girl going through puberty, one of the most significant changes that you will notice is the changes in your skin. Puberty brings an increase in hormones that can trigger an array of skin changes. For example, you may notice an increase in oil production, resulting in oily skin, breakouts, and blackheads. Many teens also experience an increase in body odor and acne due to the increase in hormones.

In addition to the above skin changes, you may also experience changes in the texture of your skin. During puberty, your skin may become more sensitive, dry, or even itchy. These changes in your skin can be due to the sudden increase in hormones, as well as a decrease in collagen production. You may also notice that your skin becomes darker in certain areas, such as the face, armpits, and groin, due to the increased production of melanin.

It is important to note that the changes in your skin during puberty are a natural process and can be managed with the right skin care routine. For example, it is important to keep your skin clean and moisturized to help maintain its balance. In addition, it is important to protect your skin from the sun, as too much exposure can lead to premature aging and skin damage.

Although the changes in your skin during puberty can be uncomfortable or even embarrassing, it is essential to remember that these changes are part of growing up. With the right skincare routine, you can ensure that your skin stays healthy and balanced throughout your teenage years.

5. Vaginal Changes

The final physical change of puberty is the development of the vagina. For a teenage girl going through puberty, vaginal changes can be both exciting and intimidating.

During puberty, the vagina begins to produce more lubrication. This is normal and necessary for sexual activity as well as other activities. As the body enters puberty, the walls of the vagina start to change, becoming thicker and more elastic. This helps to provide better protection against infection and to help the vagina be more comfortable during sexual activity.

Along with the physical changes to the vagina, the hormones that are released during puberty can affect the vagina too. As the hormones increase, the vagina will become increasingly sensitive to touch. This is why it is important for teenage girls to learn about proper hygiene and the importance of protecting the vagina from infection.

The biggest change that will occur during puberty is the onset of menarche, or the first menstrual period. This is a sign that a girl has reached sexual maturity, and that she is able to become pregnant. During menarche, the body will produce more vaginal discharge, which is a normal and natural part of the menstrual cycle.

In addition to the physical changes, teenage girls will experience a range of emotions during this time. It is important to discuss these feelings with a trusted adult to ensure that they are handled in a healthy way.

Emotional Changes

The onset of a teen girl's first period is a milestone in her life, and it can be a source of both excitement and anxiety. Here's a look at the emotional changes that may occur during this time, and how to manage them.

The first emotional change that a teen girl may experience when she starts her period is a sense of being overwhelmed. This is a normal reaction to the new and unfamiliar experience of menstruation. It can be difficult to understand the physical changes, and the sudden increase of hormones can cause intense emotions. It is important to remember that this is a normal part of growing up.

Teen girls may also experience mood swings during their period. This is due to the hormone fluctuations that occur during this time. These can range from feeling content and happy to feeling irritable or anxious. It is important to be aware of these feelings and talk to a trusted adult if they become too much to handle.

Another emotional change that can occur during this time is a feeling of insecurity. This may manifest as a fear of being judged or criticized by peers or family members. While it is normal to feel insecure during this time, it is important to remember that you are not alone. It can be helpful to talk to someone you trust about your feelings and insecurities.

Finally, a teen girl may experience a sense of loneliness during her period. This is because of the physical and emotional changes that may make it difficult to connect with others. It is important to remember that you are not the only one going through this, and that there are people who understand and are willing to help.

B. Understanding Menstruation And How to Prepare For It

Menstruation is an important part of a woman's life, and is a natural process that all women experience. As a teen girl, it is important to understand the menstrual cycle and learn how to prepare for it. This chapter will provide an overview of the menstrual cycle and offer practical tips on how to check your menstrual cycle and prepare for it as a teen girl.

What is the Menstrual Cycle?

Menstruation or the menstrual cycle is a normal part of being a teenage girl. It usually starts between the ages of 10-16 and is the body's way of preparing for pregnancy. During a menstrual cycle, the body goes through a series of hormonal changes that can cause physical and emotional changes.

The menstrual cycle begins with the first day of your period and lasts for around 28 days. During this time, the hormones oestrogen and progesterone cause the lining of the uterus to thicken. An egg is released from one of the ovaries and if the egg is not fertilized, the lining of the uterus is shed and a period starts.

It's important to be aware of the signs and symptoms of your menstrual cycle, as it can help you to understand how your body is changing. At the start of the cycle, you may experience cramps, headaches and mood swings. As the cycle progresses, you may experience swollen and tender breasts, acne, bloating and increased hunger.

Lastly, it's important to look after your mental and physical health during your menstrual cycle. This can include eating a balanced diet, exercising regularly, and talking with a doctor or health care provider if you have any concerns. Regular check-ups can also help to ensure that your menstrual cycle is normal and healthy.

How to Check Your Menstrual Cycle

To check your menstrual cycle, you should keep track of your period each month. You can use a calendar or a mobile app to track the start and end of your period. Write down the date your period starts and ends, as well as any other notable symptoms such as cramps or spotting. This will give you a better understanding of your cycle.

Second, count the days between your periods. Your cycle is the total number of days between the start of one period and the start of the next. For example, if your period starts on the first of the month and the next one starts on the seventh, then your cycle is seven days. It is important to note that some cycles can be shorter or longer than seven days, so it is important to track your cycle over several months to get an accurate picture.

Third, calculate the length of your cycle. The average cycle length is 28 days, but this can vary from person to person. To calculate your cycle length, take the total number of days between the start of each period and divide it by the number of periods. For example, if your cycle was seven days and you had four periods, then your cycle length would be 28 days.

Fourth, calculate the length of your luteal phase. The luteal phase is the time between ovulation and the start of your next period. To calculate your luteal phase, subtract the number of days from the start of your period to the day you ovulated from the total number of days in your cycle. For example, if your cycle was 28 days and you ovulated on day 14, then your luteal phase would be 14 days.

Finally, calculate your fertile window. This is the time in your cycle when you are most likely to get pregnant. The fertile window is usually six days long, starting five days before you ovulate and ending on the day of ovulation. To calculate your fertile window, take the day you ovulated and subtract five days. For example, if you ovulated on day 14, your fertile window would start on day 9 and end on day 14.

How to Prepare for Your Period

Once you know when your period is coming, there are several steps you can take to prepare for it.

1. Learn about your cycle: It's important to understand your cycle and keep track of when your period is coming. Keeping track of your cycle will help you know when to expect it and how to prepare for it.

2. Stock up on supplies. Make sure you have enough pads, tampons, or menstrual cups to last the duration of your period. It's also a good idea to keep spare supplies in case of an emergency.

3. Prepare a period kit: Put together a period kit with your supplies, as well as other items like ibuprofen, chocolate, and a hot water bottle. Having all of your supplies in one place will make it easier to access them when needed.

4. Make a plan. Decide ahead of time how you will manage your menstrual cycle, such as scheduling time out of school or work if needed.

5. Know your symptoms. Pay attention to any physical or emotional changes you experience

during your menstrual cycle so that you can prepare accordingly.

6. Know your menstrual cramps: Menstrual cramps are a normal part of the menstrual cycle, so it's important to know how to manage them. Try taking ibuprofen or other over-the-counter pain medications to help reduce cramps. You can also try activities like yoga, meditation, and hot baths to help ease your cramps.

7. Get comfortable. Wear comfortable clothes, such as breathable fabrics, that won't be restrictive during your period.

8. Stay hydrated: Drinking enough water is important for your overall health, and it's especially important during your period. Staying hydrated can help reduce bloating and cramping, as well as help your body flush out toxins.

9. Talk to someone. If you are feeling overwhelmed or need support, reach out to a friend, family member, or health care provider.

Menstruation is an important part of a woman's life and should be celebrated. As a teen girl, it is important to understand the menstrual cycle and learn how to prepare for it.

IV

Making Friends and Connecting with Others

Making friends and connecting with others is one of the most important things that you can do as a teen. It is a necessary part of growing up and developing into a well-rounded and social person. The teenage years can be a difficult time, and having a strong network of friends and connections can help you through the rough patches.

The first step to making friends and connecting with others is to put yourself out there. Join clubs or activities that interest you and make an effort to get to know the people who are involved in them. Make an introduction and strike up a discussion without being hesitant to do so. Even if the other person doesn't reciprocate, you will have made the effort, which is half the battle.

Another way to make friends and connections is to join online communities. There are a variety of online groups and forums that are specifically geared toward teens. These can be a great way to meet people with similar interests and to get advice from other teens who may be going through similar experiences as you.

When it comes to making friends and connecting with others, it is important to keep an open mind. Don't be too quick to judge people or assume that you know what they are like. Everyone is different, so take the time to get to know someone before deciding if they could be a potential friend.

Be yourself. It can be tempting to try and act like someone else in order to fit in, but this is rarely a good idea. People are drawn to those who are authentic and genuine, so don't be afraid to be yourself.

Finally, try to be a good friend to others. Don't just think about what you can get out of the friendship. Instead, focus on how you can be a supportive and attentive friend. Listen to what your friends have to say and offer advice, even if it is something as simple as giving a shoulder to cry on.

Making friends and connecting with others can be a difficult process, but it can also be incredibly rewarding. Taking the time to build relationships and create meaningful connections with others can be a great way to enrich your life and make the teenage years a bit easier.

Developing Social Skills

Social skills are essential for teenage girls to lead successful lives. Social skills enable you to form meaningful relationships, build healthy self-esteem, and gain respect from your peers. Without them, teens are more likely to experience social exclusion, depression, and anxiety.

Fortunately, social skills can be developed and improved. Teens can learn to be more assertive, confident, and empathetic. Here are some tips to help teenage girls develop their social skills.

1. Learn to Listen

Listening is one of the most important social skills for teens to learn. It's important for teens to be able to listen without judgment and to be able to ask the right questions. Listening is key to forming relationships and having meaningful conversations.

2. Improve Your Communication Skills

Communication is essential in any social situation. Teens should learn how to communicate effectively in both verbal and nonverbal ways. This includes learning how to make eye contact, use appropriate body language, and express your thoughts and feelings in a respectful manner.

3. Be Assertive

Assertiveness is the ability to express yourself confidently and respectfully. It's important for you to learn how to stand up for yourself and express your opinions without being aggressive or intimidating.

4. Show Empathy

It's important for you to be able to recognize and relate to the feelings of others. This helps to form stronger relationships and foster a sense of understanding and compassion.

5. Develop Healthy Self-Esteem

Healthy self-esteem is essential for you to feel confident in social situations. You should practice self-care and find activities that make you feel good about yourself. This will help you to feel more secure and confident in social interactions.

6. Take Risks

It is important for you to take risks and try new things. Taking risks will help you to gain confidence and develop your social skills. This could include joining a new club or trying out for a sports team.

7. Practice

The best way to improve social skills is to practice. You should practice talking to people, expressing your feelings, and participating in activities with others. This will help you to gain confidence and develop your social skills.

8. Make Eye Contact: Eye contact is an important part of having conversations and connecting with people. Making eye contact shows that you're engaged in the conversation and that you care about what the other person is saying. It also helps to build trust and foster understanding.

9. Learn to Manage Conflict: Conflict is unavoidable, but it doesn't have to be destructive.

Learning how to manage conflict in a positive way is an important part of developing social skills. This includes learning how to identify and express your feelings, how to listen to and understand the other person's perspective, and how to work together to find a solution.

Developing social skills is an important part of growing up. With these tips, teenage girls can learn how to be more assertive, confident, and empathetic. This will help you to form meaningful relationships and gain respect from your peers.

Navigating Social Media

Navigating social media as a teen girl can be intimidating and overwhelming. Social media platforms are constantly changing, creating an ever-evolving landscape for young people. With the rise of cyberbullying, it's important that teens understand the potential dangers these platforms can present and how to find a balance between enjoying the benefits that social media has to offer, while avoiding any potential pitfalls.

The first step for teen girls to navigate social media is to establish a personal set of guidelines. Think about why you are on social media and what type of content you want to post or follow. Set limits on how much time you spend on social media and when you will log on or off. Consider what information you are comfortable sharing online and what type of posts or comments you are willing to engage in. By setting personal boundaries, teens can stay safe and stay in control of their online presence.

Next, teens should be mindful of their online behavior. It's important to think twice before posting or commenting on anything, as posts and comments can often be misinterpreted or taken out of context. It's also important to remember that once something is posted online, it can often be difficult to delete it. Before posting, consider if the content is kind and respectful, and if it's something you would be comfortable having associated with your name.

In addition, it's important to be aware of cyberbullying. Cyberbullying is defined as when someone is harassed, threatened, embarrassed, or targeted online.

The best course of action if you ever become a victim of cyberbullying is to report the incident to the platform and block the harasser. If you feel comfortable, you can also reach out to a school counselor or a trusted adult for help.

Finally, it's important to be aware of privacy settings on social media platforms. Many sites allow users to customize their settings so that only people you approve can view your profile. Additionally, many apps have the ability to share your location, and it's important to be aware of this so that you can control who can see where you are.

Navigating social media as a teen girl can be challenging, but it doesn't have to be. Teens can feel certain and in control of their online experience by setting up personal rules, being attentive of behavior online, being aware of cyberbullying, and understanding how to use privacy settings.

Social media can be a great way for teens to connect with friends, share their experiences, and express themselves. With the right set of rules, teens can stay safe and enjoy the benefits social media has to offer.

V

Dealing with Peer Pressure

As a teenage girl, dealing with peer pressure can be a difficult and overwhelming experience. Peer pressure is the influence from peers to do certain things, and it is a common occurrence during adolescence. It can be beneficial when used to motivate and challenge each other in positive ways, but it can also be harmful when it influences teens to engage in risky behaviors. Being aware of the various forms of peer pressure and understanding how to respond is essential for any teenage girl.

The most common type of peer pressure is social pressure. This is when peers encourage each other to do things that are accepted in their social circle, such as going to parties, drinking alcohol, and using drugs. Social pressure can be subtle or overt, with peers trying to convince or pressure one another into engaging in activities or behaviors. It is important to be aware of this form of peer pressure and to be able to recognize it in order to make an informed decision.

Another form of peer pressure is academic pressure. This is when peers try to influence each other to get good grades or to excel in academics. Academic pressure can be beneficial when used to motivate each other to do their best, but it can also be harmful when it creates unrealistic expectations or leads to competition that is damaging to one's self-esteem. Being aware of this type of peer pressure and understanding how to respond is essential for any teenage girl.

The best way to deal with peer pressure is to be aware of it and to be confident in your own decision-making. It is important to recognize when peers are trying to influence you and to be able to stand up for yourself and your beliefs. This can be difficult, but it is essential in order to maintain a healthy sense of self.

It is also important, to be honest with your peers and to communicate openly and honestly with them. Being able to talk to your peers about your feelings and beliefs can help to build trust and understanding between you and your peers. Additionally, having supportive and understanding friends can help to create a safe space where you can feel more comfortable expressing yourself without fear of judgment or rejection.

Finally, it is critical to recognize when you are feeling overwhelmed or uncomfortable with peer pressure. Taking a step back and assessing your feelings can help to clarify your thoughts and decide what is best for you. If you need additional support, consider talking to a trusted adult or counselor.

Dealing with peer pressure can be a difficult and challenging experience for any teenage girl. However, by being aware of the various types of peer pressure and understanding how to respond, it is possible to navigate these situations in a healthy and productive way. Remember to be honest with yourself and your peers, and to trust your own judgment when it comes to making decisions.

Recognizing Negative Influences

As a teenage girl, it can be difficult to identify and avoid negative influences. From peer pressure to social media, there are many sources of negative influence that can be difficult to recognize and avoid. To successfully navigate these influences and stay on the right path, it is important to understand how to recognize and address them.

One of the most common sources of negative influence that teenage girls face is peer pressure. Peer pressure can come in many forms, from subtle comments or actions to overtly pressuring someone to do something that they don't want to do. It can be hard to recognize when peers are trying to influence you in a negative way, but it is important to be aware of the subtle signs. If your peers are making comments or suggestions that make you feel uncomfortable or pressured, it is important to take a step back and evaluate whether or not you want to do what they are suggesting.

Social media can also be a source of negative influence for teenage girls. Social media can be a great way to stay connected with friends and family, but it can also be a source of comparison, insecurity, and self-doubt. It is important to recognize when you are feeling negative emotions due to what you have seen on social media. If this happens, it can be helpful to take a break from social media or limit the amount of time that you spend on it.

Another source of negative influence for teenage girls is the media. The media often portrays unrealistic body images and ideals that can be hard to escape from. It is important to recognize when these images and messages are affecting your self-esteem and body image. It can be helpful to focus on what makes you unique and to practice self-love and acceptance.

Finally, it is important to recognize when your relationships are becoming negative influences. If you find yourself in a relationship that is damaging your self-esteem or making you feel unsafe, it is important to take steps to get out of it. It can be helpful to reach out to a trusted adult or counselor for support.

Overall, it is important for teenage girls to be aware of the sources of negative influence that they may face. From peer pressure to social media, it can be hard to recognize and avoid these influences, but it is important to be aware of how they can affect you. By understanding how to recognize and address negative influences, teenage girls can stay on the right path and make positive choices.

Creating Healthy Boundaries

Creating healthy boundaries as a teenage girl can be an important part of growing up. It's important to recognize when someone is crossing a line, and to know when to say no. Setting boundaries can help you protect your physical and emotional safety, maintain your self-respect, and establish healthy relationships with others.

One of the most important boundaries to set as a teenage girl is to know when to say "no". Many teens are pressured to do things they don't want to do, such as drinking alcohol, smoking, or engaging in sexual activities. It's important to be firm in your decision and to know your limits. If someone is pressuring you to do something that makes you feel uncomfortable, say no and remove yourself from the situation.

It's also important to establish boundaries in your relationships with friends and family. This can include setting limits on how much time you spend with them, or setting boundaries on the kinds of topics that are off-limits in conversations. You should also be mindful of how much personal information you share with people and how much access they have to your social media accounts.

In addition to relationships with peers, it's important to create boundaries with adults in your life, such as teachers, coaches, and employers. This includes setting limits on the kinds of topics that are off-limits in conversations, as well as respecting their authority and not speaking to them in a disrespectful way.

Creating healthy boundaries also includes setting limits on technology usage. This includes setting limits on the amount of time you spend on your phone or other devices, as well as setting rules about what kinds of content you're allowed to access.

Finally, it's important to create boundaries for yourself. This can include setting limits on the amount of time you spend on activities that don't enrich your life, or setting limits on how much time you spend in front of a screen. It's also important to set limits on how much energy you give to relationships that don't bring you joy or benefit your life in some way.

Creating healthy boundaries as a teenage girl can be a difficult process, but it's important for protecting your mental and physical health and establishing healthy relationships with others. Setting boundaries can help you maintain your self-respect and create a sense of safety and security in your life.

VI

Overcoming Challenges and Difficult Situations

Being a teenage girl can be a difficult time in life. As young adults, teenage girls are trying to navigate the transition from childhood to adulthood. With so many competing pressures from family, peers, school, and society, it can be difficult to know how to deal with difficult situations. However, it is possible to develop the skills and strategies needed to overcome these challenges and succeed.

First and foremost, it is important to remember that every person is unique and has different strengths and weaknesses. It's important to focus on what you do well and use those strengths to help you cope with the challenges you may face. When faced with a difficult situation, try to identify what you can control and what you can't control. By recognizing your own limitations and understanding the things you can't change, you can better manage the situation.

It is also important to learn how to manage stress and anxiety. When feeling overwhelmed, take a step back and take a deep breath. Focus on calming your body and mind so you can think clearly and make decisions that are best for you. It is also beneficial to practice relaxation techniques such as yoga, meditation, and deep breathing.

Maintaining a strong support system is also essential for overcoming difficult situations. Surrounding yourself with people who believe in you and are willing to listen and offer guidance can make all the difference. Whether it be family, friends, mentors, or teachers, having people who you trust and feel comfortable talking to can help provide perspective and encouragement when needed.

Finally, it is important to practice self-care. Taking care of your physical and mental health is essential for managing difficult situations. Make sure to get enough sleep and exercise, eat healthy foods, and take time for yourself each day. Prioritizing your own well-being can help to provide a sense of stability and reassurance during difficult times.

No matter what challenges or difficult situations teenage girls may face, it is possible to overcome them. By recognizing your own strengths and limitations, managing stress and anxiety, developing a strong support system, and practicing self-care, you can gain the skills and strategies needed to navigate difficult times. With a positive attitude, determination, and resilience, teenage girls can reach their full potential and achieve success.

Identifying Your Strengths

As a teen girl, it's important to understand and identify your strengths. Knowing your strengths can help you make better decisions, become more self-confident, and set yourself up for success. Whether it's in school, relationships, or work, having a clear sense of your talents can help you feel more in control of your life.

The first step in identifying your strengths is to take some time to think about what you're good at. This could include school activities, hobbies, sports, and any other areas where you excel. Consider things that come easily to you and that you enjoy doing. List your advantages by spending some time doing so.

Once you have a list of your strengths, it's time to think more deeply about what they mean to you. What do your strengths say about you? Are there any common themes or values that connect them? Do any of your strengths offer insight into your passions or interests?

After you've identified your strengths, it's important to start using them. Think about how you can use your strengths to set yourself up for success and make positive changes in your life. For example, if you're a great writer, you might take a writing class or start a blog. If you're good at math, you could consider taking a math course or tutoring other students.

Identifying and using your strengths can also help you build self-confidence. When you use your strengths to accomplish something, it can give you a sense of pride and accomplishment. This can help lead to more self-confidence over time.

Finally, identifying your strengths can help you make better decisions in other areas of your life. It can help you identify career paths that fit your skills and interests. It can also help you decide how to use your free time and set yourself up for success.

Overall, recognizing and using your strengths can be a great way to take control of your life as a teen girl. It can help you become more confident and make better decisions. It can also give you insight into your passions and interests. Take some time to think about what your strengths are, how you can use them, and how they can help you set yourself up for success

Developing Coping Strategies

As a teenage girl, life can be full of challenges and difficult situations. From balancing school work and extracurricular activities, to dealing with social pressures and family dynamics, there is no denying that teenage life can be overwhelming at times. As a result, it's important to develop coping strategies to help you manage the stress and anxiety that can come with these situations. The following advice can help you accomplish that.

1. Create a Personal Toolbox

One of the most important things you can do to cope with challenging situations is to create a "toolbox" of coping strategies. This toolbox should contain activities or techniques that help you relax and reduce stress. Examples of activities you may want to include in your toolbox are yoga, meditation, journaling, deep breathing, walking, listening to music, and engaging in creative pursuits. Having a variety of activities that you can turn to in times of stress can help you stay calm and grounded.

2. Talk to Someone

It's important to have a supportive network of people you can turn to when you're feeling overwhelmed. Don't be afraid to reach out to family members, friends, teachers, or counselors to talk about your feelings and struggles. Talking to someone you trust can help you gain perspective and come up with solutions that can help you manage difficult situations.

3. Set Boundaries

It's also important to set boundaries and prioritize your mental health. Don't be afraid to say "no" to activities or people that don't serve you. Taking a break from social media or other activities that can add to your stress can help you find balance and reduce anxiety.

4. Exercise – Exercise is a great way to reduce stress and improve your mood. Going for a run, playing a sport, or doing yoga can help to release endorphins and reduce anxiety.

5. Take Breaks – Taking breaks throughout the day can help to clear your mind and give you time to relax. Whether it's taking a few minutes to stretch, going for a walk, or listening to music, taking breaks can help to reduce stress.

6. Get Enough Sleep – Making sure to get enough sleep is important for your physical and mental health. Getting enough sleep can help to improve your focus and reduce stress.

7. Connect with Nature – Getting outside in nature can be a great way to reduce stress. Going for a walk in a park, sitting by a lake, or exploring a nearby trail can help to clear your mind and give you a break from the stress of everyday life.

8. Take Time to Unplug – With the pressures of social media and technology, it's important to take time to unplug. Taking a break from your phone and other devices can help to reduce stress and give you time to focus on yourself.

9. Talk to a Mentor – If you don't feel comfortable talking to a friend or family member, talking to a mentor can be a great way to get an outside perspective and gain advice.

10. Volunteer – Volunteering can be a great way to reduce stress and give back to your community. Taking time to volunteer for a cause you care about can help to give you a sense of purpose and satisfaction.

Developing coping strategies can help you manage the stress and anxiety that can come with being a teenage girl. Remember to create a personal toolbox of activities that can help you relax, talk to someone you trust, set boundaries, practice self-care, and practice mindfulness.

VII

Preparing for Your Future

As a teenage girl, it is important to begin preparing for your future. Whether you are in high school or college, having a solid plan for your future will help you to achieve your goals and reach your full potential. Here are some tips for preparing for your future as a teen girl.

First, identify your goals and dreams. What do you want to accomplish in life? What do you plan to do when you're older? Do you have any particular job interests? Write down your responses after giving these questions some thought. Having a clear direction for your future will help you focus your energy and resources on the right activities and choices.

Second, create a plan. Once you've identified your goals, create a plan to help you reach them. This might include researching the requirements for your desired career, creating a timeline with deadlines, and making a list of potential schools and programs to apply to. It's important to be realistic and to create a plan that is achievable.

Third, get involved in extracurricular activities. Participating in activities outside of school is a great way to gain experience, meet new people, and develop important skills. Look for programs and clubs related to your interests and get involved. This will help you gain insight into your future career and give you the opportunity to demonstrate your leadership abilities.

Fourth, take advantage of learning opportunities. Take classes and workshops related to your desired career. This will give you an edge when applying to college or seeking a job. Additionally, you can participate in online forums and communities relating to your hobbies. Reading books, listening to podcasts, and attending seminars are also great ways to increase your knowledge and develop your skills.

Finally, stay organized. Keeping track of deadlines, tasks, and important documents can be a challenge. Set up a system for organizing your papers, emails, and other important information. Establish a regular routine for completing tasks and create reminders for due dates. This will help you stay on track and prevent you from missing important opportunities.

Preparing for your future as a teenage girl can seem daunting at first, but it doesn't have to be. With the right plan and dedication, you can achieve your goals and create a successful future for yourself. Good luck!

Setting Goals

As a teen girl, setting goals is an important part of growing up and creating a bright future for yourself. With the right goals in place, you can create a plan for success and work toward achieving your dreams.

Setting goals is a great way to stay motivated and focused on the things that you want to accomplish. It can also help you stay on track and make sure that you're taking steps to reach your desired destination.

When setting goals, it's important to think about what's important to you. Whether it's academic, career, or personal goals, make sure that you're setting goals that you truly want to accomplish, and that are within your reach.

Start by writing down your goals. Writing down your goals can help you stay organized and give you a sense of clarity. It can also help you keep track of your progress and know when you've reached a goal you set for yourself.

When setting goals, it's important to be specific. Make sure that you're writing down measurable goals that you can track and measure your progress against. Having a clear vision of what you want to accomplish with your goals can help you stay focused and motivated.

Create a timeline and action plan for each goal. Having a timeline and action plan can help you stay on track and on top of things. Make sure you're realistic about the timeline and action plan you create, as this will help you stay on track and make sure you're taking the necessary steps to reach your goal.

Reward yourself for meeting your goals. When you're working hard toward something, it can be easy to forget to reward yourself. Whether it's a small reward or something bigger, make sure to reward yourself when you reach a goal that you set for yourself.

Finally, don't be afraid to adjust your goals. Life doesn't always go according to plan, so it's important to be flexible and adjust your goals as needed. Don't be afraid to change your goals or alter your timeline or action plan if something isn't working out the way you planned it.

Setting goals is an important part of being a teen girl, as it can help you stay motivated and focused on the things that are important to you. With the right goals in place and a plan for success, you can work toward achieving your dreams and creating a bright future

Creating a Plan for College and Beyond

As a teen girl, it is important to have a plan for college and beyond. Making a plan for the future can be daunting, but it is essential to have a plan in order to help set yourself up for success down the road. Here are some tips for creating a plan for college and beyond as a teen girl.

1. Start by researching colleges and universities that you are interested in attending. Determine what type of degree you want to pursue and what types of schools offer that degree. Look into the admissions requirements and tuition costs of each

school. Take an assessment of your current academic abilities and find out what type of scholarships are available.

2. Develop a timeline for when you want to complete your degree. Make sure that you are realistic about your goals and that you plan ahead for any additional courses or certifications that you may need. Make sure to include time for studying and taking standardized tests such as the SAT or ACT.

3. Consider the financial implications of your plan. Determine how much money you will need for tuition, fees, books, and other expenses. Research options for student loans, grants, and scholarships, and create a budget for yourself.

4. Think about what you want to do after college. Research career paths that interest you and figure out what type of education you may need for a specific job. Look into internships or apprenticeship programs that can help you build experience in a chosen field.

5. Consider how you will stay focused and motivated throughout the process. Set short-term and long-term goals for yourself and keep a record of your progress. Get involved with

activities that will help you develop skills and build relationships with peers.

Conclusion

Teen Girl's Survival Guide is an invaluable resource for young women entering their teenage years. In this book I try my best to provide advice on how to make friends, build confidence, avoid peer pressure, overcome challenges, prepare for the future, and just about everything in between through my past experiences and previous encounters.

I believe this guide is essential for all women and not just for only young girls as it provides insight and guidance on navigating the tumultuous teenage years. It will allow you to develop the necessary skills and tools to succeed in life and become confident, successful women.

In conclusion as a woman you need to remember that life will always have it's up and downs, it's the ability to master the skills you need to help you during these though times that'll make you who you are just the way you need to be.

I hope you take the skills you've learnt from this book and start implementing them in your day to day life. If this book has been an inspiration or has helped you out in any way I would really love

to hear how as my joy as a writer is knowing that my books have positively impacted someone's life. Please kindly let me know by visiting and leaving a few positive words here
www.amazon.com/review/create-review/B0BSMW7JCV

Thank you for making the decision to learn about special survival skills you need as a developing young woman.